Contents

Cookies

Choco-Peanut Butter-Brickle Cookies

    1 (14-ounce) can EAGLE BRAND® Sweetened Condensed Milk
       (NOT evaporated milk)
    1 cup crunchy peanut butter
    2 eggs
    1 teaspoon vanilla extract
  1½ cups all-purpose flour
    1 teaspoon baking soda
    ½ teaspoon baking powder
    ½ teaspoon salt
    1 cup (6 ounces) semisweet chocolate chips
    1 cup chocolate-covered toffee bits or almond brickle chips

1. Preheat oven to 350°F. In large bowl, beat EAGLE BRAND®, peanut butter, eggs and vanilla until well blended.

2. In medium bowl, combine flour, baking soda, baking powder and salt. Add to peanut butter mixture; beat until blended. Stir in chocolate chips and toffee bits. Drop by heaping tablespoonfuls onto lightly greased baking sheets.

3. Bake 12 minutes or until lightly browned. Cool slightly on baking sheets; remove to wire racks to cool completely.

Makes 3 dozen cookies

Prep Time: *15 minutes*
Bake Time: *12 minutes*

Chocolate Chip Treasure Cookies

1½ **cups graham cracker crumbs**
½ **cup all-purpose flour**
2 **teaspoons baking powder**
1 **(14-ounce) can EAGLE BRAND® Sweetened Condensed Milk (NOT evaporated milk)**
½ **cup (1 stick) butter or margarine, softened**
2 **cups (12 ounces) semisweet chocolate chips**
1⅓ **cups flaked coconut**
1 **cup chopped walnuts**

1. Preheat oven to 375°F. In small bowl, combine graham cracker crumbs, flour and baking powder.

2. In large bowl, beat EAGLE BRAND® and butter until smooth.

3. Add crumb mixture; mix well. Stir in chocolate chips, coconut and walnuts.

4. Drop by rounded tablespoonfuls onto ungreased baking sheets. Bake 9 to 10 minutes or until lightly browned. Cool. Store loosely covered at room temperature.   *Makes about 3 dozen cookies*

Prep Time: 10 minutes
Bake Time: 9 to 10 minutes

Coconut Macaroons

1 (14-ounce) can EAGLE BRAND® Sweetened Condensed Milk (NOT evaporated milk)
1 egg white, whipped
2 teaspoons vanilla extract
1½ teaspoons almond extract
1 (14-ounce) package flaked coconut

1. Preheat oven to 325°F. Line baking sheets with foil; grease and flour foil. Set aside.

2. In large bowl, combine EAGLE BRAND®, egg white, extracts and coconut; mix well. Drop by rounded teaspoonfuls onto prepared baking sheets; slightly flatten each mound with a spoon.

3. Bake 15 to 17 minutes or until lightly browned around edges. Immediately remove from baking sheets (macaroons will stick if allowed to cool on baking sheets); cool on wire racks. Store loosely covered at room temperature. *Makes about 4 dozen cookies*

Prep Time: *10 minutes*
Bake Time: *15 to 17 minutes*

Cinnamon Chip Gems

- 1 cup (2 sticks) butter or margarine, softened
- 2 (3-ounce) packages cream cheese, softened
- 2 cups all-purpose flour
- 1/2 cup sugar
- 1/3 cup ground toasted almonds
- 2 eggs
- 1 (14-ounce) can EAGLE BRAND® Sweetened Condensed Milk (NOT evaporated milk)
- 1 teaspoon vanilla extract
- 1 1/3 cups cinnamon baking chips, divided

1. In large bowl, beat butter and cream cheese until well blended. Stir in flour, sugar and almonds. Cover; chill about 1 hour.

2. Divide dough into 4 equal parts. Shape each part into 12 smooth balls. Place each ball in small ungreased muffin cup (1 3/4 inches in diameter); press evenly on bottom and up side of each cup.

3. Preheat oven to 375°F. In small bowl, beat eggs. Add EAGLE BRAND® and vanilla; mix well. Place 7 cinnamon baking chips in bottom of each muffin cup; generously fill three-fourths full with EAGLE BRAND® mixture.

4. Bake 18 to 20 minutes or until tops are puffed and just beginning to turn golden brown. Cool 3 minutes. Sprinkle about 10 chips on top of filling. Cool completely in pan on wire rack.

5. Remove from pan using small metal spatula or sharp knife. Cool completely. Store tightly covered at room temperature.

Makes 4 dozen gems

Tip: For a pretty presentation, line the muffin pan with colorful paper baking cups before pressing the dough into the muffin cups.

Prep Time: 20 minutes
Chill Time: 1 hour
Bake Time: 18 to 20 minutes

Chocolate Peanut Butter Chip Cookies

8 (1-ounce) squares semisweet chocolate
3 tablespoons butter or margarine
1 (14-ounce) can EAGLE BRAND® Sweetened Condensed Milk (NOT evaporated milk)
2 cups biscuit baking mix
1 egg
1 teaspoon vanilla extract
1 cup (6 ounces) peanut butter-flavored chips

1. Preheat oven to 350°F. In large saucepan over low heat melt chocolate and butter with EAGLE BRAND®; remove from heat.

2. Add biscuit mix, egg and vanilla; with mixer, beat until smooth and well blended. Let mixture cool to room temperature. Stir in peanut butter chips.

3. Drop by rounded teaspoonfuls onto ungreased baking sheets. Bake 6 to 8 minutes or until tops are lightly crusted. Cool. Store leftovers tightly covered at room temperature.

Makes about 4 dozen cookies

Prep Time: *20 minutes*
Bake Time: *6 to 8 minutes*

Macaroon Kisses

1 (14-ounce) can EAGLE BRAND® Sweetened Condensed Milk (NOT evaporated milk)
1 egg white, whipped
2 teaspoons vanilla extract
1½ teaspoons almond extract
1 (14-ounce) package flaked coconut
48 solid milk chocolate candy kisses, stars or drops, unwrapped

1. Preheat oven to 325°F. Line baking sheets with foil; grease and flour foil. Set aside.

2. In large bowl, combine EAGLE BRAND®, egg white, extracts and coconut; mix well. Drop by rounded teaspoonfuls onto prepared baking sheets; slightly flatten each mound with a spoon.

3. Bake 15 to 17 minutes or until lightly browned around edges. Remove from oven. Immediately press candy kiss, star or drop in center of each macaroon. Remove from baking sheets (macaroons will stick if allowed to cool on baking sheets); cool on wire racks. Store loosely covered at room temperature.

Makes 4 dozen cookies

Cut-Out Cookies

3½ cups all-purpose flour
2 teaspoons baking powder
¼ teaspoon salt
1 (14-ounce) can EAGLE BRAND® Sweetened Condensed Milk
  (NOT evaporated milk)
¾ cup (1½ sticks) butter or margarine, softened
2 eggs
1 tablespoon vanilla extract
  Colored sugar sprinkles (optional)
  Powdered Sugar Glaze (page 11, optional)

1. In small bowl, combine flour, baking powder and salt; set aside.

2. In large bowl with mixer on low speed, beat EAGLE BRAND®, butter, eggs and vanilla until just combined. Beat on medium speed 1 minute until smooth. Add flour mixture; beat on low speed until combined. (If using hand-held mixer, use wooden spoon to add last portion of flour mixture.)

3. Divide dough into thirds. Wrap and chill dough 2 hours or until easy to handle.

4. Preheat oven to 350°F. On lightly floured surface, roll out one portion of dough to ⅛-inch thickness. Cut out shapes with floured cookie cutters. Reroll as necessary to use all dough. Place cut-outs 1 inch apart on ungreased baking sheets. Sprinkle with colored sugar (optional).

5. Bake 9 to 11 minutes or until very lightly browned around edges (do not overbake). Cool. Glaze and decorate (optional). Remove cookies to wire racks. Store leftovers loosely covered at room temperature.   *Makes 5½ dozen cookies*

Tip: Freeze Cut-Out Cookies in a tightly sealed container.

Prep Time: 15 minutes
Chill Time: 2 hours
Bake Time: 9 to 11 minutes

Powdered Sugar Glaze

- **2 cups sifted powdered sugar**
- **½ teaspoon vanilla extract**
- **2 tablespoons milk or whipping cream**
- **Food coloring (optional)**

Combine sugar and vanilla, adding just enough milk to make glaze consistency. Add food coloring (optional) to tint glaze.

Easy Peanut Butter Cookies

**1 (14-ounce) can EAGLE BRAND® Sweetened Condensed Milk
(NOT evaporated milk)**
1 to 1¼ cups peanut butter
1 egg
1 teaspoon vanilla extract
2 cups biscuit baking mix
Granulated sugar

1. In large bowl, beat EAGLE BRAND®, peanut butter, egg and vanilla until smooth. Add biscuit mix; mix well. Chill at least 1 hour.

2. Preheat oven to 350°F. Shape dough into 1-inch balls. Roll in sugar. Place 2 inches apart on ungreased baking sheets. Flatten with fork in criss-cross pattern.

3. Bake 6 to 8 minutes or until lightly browned (do not overbake). Cool. Store tightly covered at room temperature.

Makes about 5 dozen cookies

Peanut Blossom Cookies: Make dough as directed above. Shape into 1-inch balls and roll in sugar; do not flatten. Bake as directed above. Immediately after baking, press solid milk chocolate candy kiss in center of each cookie.

Peanut Butter & Jelly Gems: Make dough as directed above. Shape into 1-inch balls and roll in sugar; do not flatten. Press thumb in center of each ball of dough; fill with jelly, jam or preserves. Proceed as directed above.

Any-Way-You-Like 'em Cookies: Stir 1 cup semisweet chocolate chips, chopped peanuts, raisins or flaked coconut into dough. Proceed as directed above.

***Prep Time:** 10 minutes*
***Chill Time:** 1 hour*
***Bake Time:** 6 to 8 minutes*

Bars & Brownies

Streusel Caramel Bars

   2 cups all-purpose flour
   ¾ cup firmly packed light brown sugar
   1 egg, beaten
   ¾ cup (1½ sticks) cold butter or margarine, divided
   ¾ cup chopped nuts
   24 caramels, unwrapped
   1 (14-ounce) can EAGLE BRAND® Sweetened Condensed Milk
       (NOT evaporated milk)

1. Preheat oven to 350°F. In large bowl, combine flour, brown sugar and egg; cut in ½ cup butter until crumbly. Stir in nuts.

2. Reserve 2 cups crumb mixture. Press remaining crumb mixture firmly on bottom of greased 13×9-inch baking pan. Bake 15 minutes.

3. In heavy saucepan over low heat, melt caramels and remaining ¼ cup butter with EAGLE BRAND®. Pour over prepared crust. Top with reserved crumb mixture.

4. Bake 20 minutes or until bubbly. Cool. Chill if desired. Cut into bars. Store loosely covered at room temperature.

Makes 2 to 3 dozen bars

Chocolate Caramel Bars: Melt 2 (1-ounce) squares unsweetened chocolate with caramels, butter and EAGLE BRAND®. Proceed as above.

Prep Time: 25 minutes
Bake Time: 35 minutes

Fudge Topped Brownies

2 cups sugar
1 cup (2 sticks) butter or margarine, melted
1 cup all-purpose flour
⅔ cup unsweetened cocoa
½ teaspoon baking powder
2 eggs
½ cup milk
3 teaspoons vanilla extract, divided
1 cup chopped nuts (optional)
2 cups (12 ounces) semisweet chocolate chips
1 (14-ounce) can EAGLE BRAND® Sweetened Condensed Milk
    (NOT evaporated milk)
Dash salt

1. Preheat oven to 350°F. In large bowl, combine sugar, butter, flour, cocoa, baking powder, eggs, milk and 1½ teaspoons vanilla; mix well. Stir in nuts (optional).

2. Spread in greased 13×9-inch baking pan. Bake 40 minutes or until brownies begin to pull away from sides of pan.

3. In heavy saucepan over low heat, melt chocolate chips with EAGLE BRAND®, remaining 1½ teaspoons vanilla and salt. Remove from heat.

4. Immediately spread over hot brownies. Cool. Chill if desired. Cut into bars. Store covered at room temperature.

Makes 3 to 3½ dozen brownies

Prep Time: *10 minutes*
Bake Time: *40 minutes*

Double Delicious Cookie Bars

1½ cups graham cracker crumbs
½ cup (1 stick) butter or margarine, melted
**1 (14-ounce) can EAGLE BRAND® Sweetened Condensed Milk
    (NOT evaporated milk)**
1 cup (6 ounces) semisweet chocolate chips*
1 cup (6 ounces) peanut butter-flavored chips*

**Butterscotch-flavored chips or white chocolate chips can be substituted
for the semisweet chocolate chips and/or the peanut butter-flavored chips.*

1. Preheat oven to 350°F (325°F for glass dish). In small bowl,
combine graham cracker crumbs and butter; mix well. Press
crumb mixture firmly on bottom of 13×9-inch baking pan.

2. Pour EAGLE BRAND® evenly over crumb mixture. Layer evenly
with chocolate chips and peanut butter chips; press down firmly
with fork.

3. Bake 25 to 30 minutes or until lightly browned. Cool. Chill if
desired. Cut into bars. Store leftovers covered at room temperature.

Makes 2 to 3 dozen bars

***Prep Time:** 10 minutes*
***Bake Time:** 25 to 30 minutes*

Chocolate Almond Bars

1½ **cups all-purpose flour**
⅔ **cup sugar**
¾ **cup (1½ sticks) cold butter or margarine**
1½ **cups semisweet chocolate chips, divided**
1 **(14-ounce) can EAGLE BRAND® Sweetened Condensed Milk**
  (NOT evaporated milk)
1 **egg**
2 **cups almonds, toasted and chopped**
½ **teaspoon almond extract**
1 **teaspoon solid shortening**

1. Preheat oven to 350°F. In large bowl, combine flour and sugar; cut in butter until crumbly. Press firmly on bottom of ungreased 13×9-inch baking pan. Bake 20 minutes or until lightly browned.

2. In medium saucepan over low heat, melt 1 cup chocolate chips with EAGLE BRAND®. Remove from heat; cool slightly. Beat in egg. Stir in almonds and extract. Spread over baked crust.

3. Bake 25 minutes or until set. Cool.

4. Melt remaining ½ cup chocolate chips with shortening; drizzle over bars. Chill 10 minutes or until set. Cut into bars. Store covered at room temperature.   *Makes 2 to 3 dozen bars*

Chocolate Nut Bars

1¾ cups graham cracker crumbs
½ cup (1 stick) butter or margarine, melted
2 cups (12 ounces) semisweet chocolate chips, divided
1 (14-ounce) can EAGLE BRAND® Sweetened Condensed Milk
(NOT evaporated milk)
1 teaspoon vanilla extract
1 cup chopped nuts

1. Preheat oven to 375°F. In medium bowl, combine graham cracker crumbs and butter; press firmly on bottom of ungreased 13×9-inch baking pan. Bake 8 minutes. Reduce oven temperature to 350°F.

2. In small saucepan over low heat, melt 1 cup chocolate chips with EAGLE BRAND® and vanilla. Spread chocolate mixture over hot crust. Top with remaining 1 cup chocolate chips and nuts; press down firmly.

3. Bake 25 to 30 minutes. Cool. Chill if desired. Cut into bars. Store loosely covered at room temperature.   *Makes 2 to 3 dozen bars*

Prep Time: *10 minutes*
Bake Time: *33 to 38 minutes*

Golden Peanut Butter Bars

    2 cups all-purpose flour
    ¾ cup firmly packed light brown sugar
    1 egg, beaten
    ½ cup (1 stick) cold butter or margarine
    1 cup chopped peanuts
    1 (14-ounce) can EAGLE BRAND® Sweetened Condensed Milk
        (NOT evaporated milk)
    ½ cup peanut butter
    1 teaspoon vanilla extract

1. Preheat oven to 350°F. In large bowl, combine flour, brown sugar and egg; cut in butter until crumbly. Stir in peanuts. Reserve 2 cups crumb mixture. Press remaining mixture on bottom of 13×9-inch baking pan. Bake 15 minutes or until lightly browned.

2. In large bowl with mixer, beat EAGLE BRAND®, peanut butter and vanilla. Spread over prepared crust; top with reserved crumb mixture.

3. Bake 25 minutes longer or until lightly browned. Cool. Chill if desired. Cut into bars. Store leftovers covered at room temperature.

Makes 2 to 3 dozen bars

Prep Time: 20 minutes
Bake Time: 40 minutes

Cheesecake-Topped Brownies

- 1 (19.5- or 22-ounce) package fudge brownie mix
- 1 (8-ounce) package cream cheese, softened
- 2 tablespoons butter or margarine, softened
- 1 tablespoon cornstarch
- 1 (14-ounce) can EAGLE BRAND® Sweetened Condensed Milk
  (NOT evaporated milk)
- 1 egg
- 2 teaspoons vanilla extract
  Ready-to-spread chocolate frosting (optional)

1. Preheat oven to 350°F. Prepare brownie mix as package directs. Spread in well-greased 13×9-inch baking pan.

2. In large bowl, beat cream cheese, butter and cornstarch until fluffy. Gradually beat in EAGLE BRAND®, egg and vanilla until smooth. Spoon cheesecake mixture evenly over brownie batter.

3. Bake 45 minutes or until top is lightly browned. Cool. Spread with frosting (optional). Cut into bars. Store leftovers covered in refrigerator.

Makes 3 to 3½ dozen brownies

Prep Time: 20 minutes
Bake Time: 45 minutes

Pecan Pie Bars

 2 cups all-purpose flour
 ¼ cup firmly packed brown sugar
 ½ cup (1 stick) cold butter
 1½ cups chopped pecans
 1 (14-ounce) can EAGLE BRAND® Sweetened Condensed Milk
   (NOT evaporated milk)
 3 eggs, beaten
 2 tablespoons lemon juice

1. Preheat oven to 350°F. In medium bowl, combine flour and brown sugar; cut in butter until crumbly.

2. Press mixture on bottom of 13×9-inch baking pan. Bake 10 to 15 minutes or until lightly browned.

3. In large bowl, combine pecans, EAGLE BRAND®, eggs and lemon juice; pour over crust.

4. Bake 25 minutes or until filling is set. Cool. Chill if desired. Cut into bars. Store covered at room temperature.

Makes about 3 dozen bars

Prep Time: *15 minutes*
Bake Time: *35 to 40 minutes*

Lemon Crumb Bars

1 (18.25- or 18.5-ounce) package lemon or yellow cake mix
½ cup (1 stick) butter or margarine, softened
1 egg
2 cups finely crushed saltine crackers
1 (14-ounce) can EAGLE BRAND® Sweetened Condensed Milk
(NOT evaporated milk)
½ cup lemon juice
3 egg yolks

1. Preheat oven to 350°F. In large bowl, combine cake mix, butter and 1 egg with mixer until crumbly. Stir in cracker crumbs. Reserve 2 cups crumb mixture. Press remaining crumb mixture firmly on bottom of greased 13×9-inch baking pan. Bake 15 to 20 minutes or until golden.

2. With mixer or wire whisk, beat EAGLE BRAND®, lemon juice and 3 egg yolks. Spread evenly over prepared crust. Top with reserved crumb mixture.

3. Bake 20 minutes longer or until set and top is golden. Cool. Cut into bars. Store leftovers covered in refrigerator.

Makes 2 to 3 dozen bars

Prep Time: *15 minutes*
Bake Time: *35 to 40 minutes*

Brownie Mint Sundae Squares

1 (19.5- or 22-ounce family size) package fudge brownie mix
¾ cup coarsely chopped walnuts
1 (14-ounce) can EAGLE BRAND® Sweetened Condensed Milk
   (NOT evaporated milk)
2 teaspoons peppermint extract
4 to 6 drops green food coloring (optional)
2 cups (1 pint) whipping cream, whipped
½ cup miniature semisweet chocolate chips
   Hot fudge sauce or chocolate-flavored syrup (optional)

1. Prepare brownie mix as package directs; stir in walnuts. Spread in foil-lined and greased 13×9-inch baking pan. Bake as directed. Cool completely.

2. In large bowl, combine EAGLE BRAND®, peppermint extract and food coloring (optional). Fold in whipped cream and chocolate chips. Spoon over brownie layer.

3. Cover; freeze 6 hours or until firm. To serve, lift brownies from pan with foil; cut into squares. Serve with hot fudge sauce (optional). Freeze leftovers. *Makes 10 to 12 servings*

Prep Time: *20 minutes*
Freeze Time: *6 hours*

Fudge-Filled Bars

    2 cups (12 ounces) semisweet chocolate chips
    2 tablespoons butter or margarine
    1 (14-ounce) can EAGLE BRAND® Sweetened Condensed Milk
        (NOT evaporated milk)
    2 teaspoons vanilla extract
    2 (16-ounce) packages refrigerated cookie dough (oatmeal-
        chocolate chip, chocolate chip or sugar cookie dough)

1. Preheat oven to 350°F. In heavy saucepan over medium heat, melt chocolate chips, butter and EAGLE BRAND®, stirring often. Remove from heat; stir in vanilla. Cool 15 minutes.

2. Using floured hands, press 1½ packages of cookie dough into ungreased 15×10-inch baking pan. Pour cooled chocolate mixture evenly over dough. Crumble remaining dough over chocolate mixture.

3. Bake 25 to 30 minutes. Cool. Chill if desired. Cut into bars. Store covered at room temperature.   *Makes 4 dozen bars*

Helpful Hint: If you want to trim the fat in any EAGLE BRAND® recipe, just use EAGLE BRAND® Fat Free or Low Fat Sweetened Condensed Milk instead of the original EAGLE BRAND®.

Prep Time: 20 minutes
Bake Time: 25 to 30 minutes

No-Bake Fudgy Brownies

1 (14-ounce) can EAGLE BRAND® Sweetened Condensed Milk (NOT evaporated milk)

2 (1-ounce) squares unsweetened chocolate, chopped

1 teaspoon vanilla extract

2 cups plus 2 tablespoons finely crushed chocolate wafer cookies (about 25 cookies), divided

¼ cup miniature candy-coated milk chocolate pieces or chopped nuts

1. In medium saucepan over low heat, combine EAGLE BRAND® and chocolate; cook and stir just until boiling. Reduce heat; cook and stir for 2 to 3 minutes more or until mixture thickens. Remove from heat; stir in vanilla.

2. Stir in 2 cups cookie crumbs. Spread evenly in greased or foil-lined 8-inch square baking pan. Sprinkle with remaining cookie crumbs and chocolate pieces; press down gently with back of spoon.

3. Cover and chill 4 hours or until firm. Turn brownies onto cutting board; peel off foil and cut into squares. Store covered in refrigerator.

Makes 2 to 3 dozen brownies

Prep Time: *10 minutes*
Chill Time: *4 hours*

Butterscotch Apple Squares

¼ **cup (½ stick) butter or margarine**
1½ **cups graham cracker crumbs**
2 **small all-purpose apples, peeled and chopped (about 1¼ cups)**
1 **cup (6 ounces) butterscotch-flavored chips**
1 **(14-ounce) can EAGLE BRAND® Sweetened Condensed Milk**
   (NOT evaporated milk)
1⅓ **cups flaked coconut**
1 **cup chopped nuts**

1. Preheat oven to 350°F (325°F for glass dish). In 13×9-inch baking pan, melt butter in oven. Sprinkle graham cracker crumbs evenly over butter; top with apples.

2. In heavy saucepan over medium heat, melt butterscotch chips with EAGLE BRAND®. Pour butterscotch mixture evenly over apples. Top with coconut and nuts; press down firmly.

3. Bake 25 to 30 minutes or until lightly browned. Cool. Cut into squares. Garnish as desired. Store leftovers covered in refrigerator.

Makes 1 dozen squares

Prep Time: *15 minutes*
Bake Time: *25 to 30 minutes*

Cheesecakes

Chocolate Mint Cheesecake Bars

2 cups finely crushed creme-filled chocolate sandwich cookies
(about 24 cookies)
½ cup (1 stick) butter or margarine, melted
1 (8-ounce) package cream cheese, softened
1 (14-ounce) can EAGLE BRAND® Sweetened Condensed Milk
(NOT evaporated milk)
2 eggs
1 tablespoon peppermint extract
½ cup semisweet chocolate chips
2 teaspoons shortening
14 thin crème de menthe candies, chopped

1. Preheat oven to 325°F. In medium bowl, combine cookie crumbs and butter; blend well. Press crumb mixture firmly on bottom of ungreased 9-inch square baking pan. Bake 6 minutes. Cool.

2. In medium bowl, beat cream cheese until fluffy. Gradually beat in EAGLE BRAND®, eggs and peppermint extract until smooth. Spread over cooled cookie base. Bake 25 to 30 minutes. Cool 20 minutes; chill.

3. Just before serving, in heavy saucepan over low heat, melt chocolate chips and shortening. Drizzle over chilled cheesecake bars. Sprinkle with chopped crème de menthe candies. Cut into bars. Store leftovers covered in refrigerator.   *Makes 1½ to 2 dozen bars*

Prep Time: 15 minutes
Bake Time: 31 to 36 minutes

Maple Pumpkin Cheesecake

1¼ cups graham cracker crumbs
¼ cup sugar
¼ cup (½ stick) butter or margarine, melted
3 (8-ounce) packages cream cheese, softened
1 (14-ounce) can EAGLE BRAND® Sweetened Condensed Milk
    (NOT evaporated milk)
1 (15-ounce) can pumpkin (2 cups)
3 eggs
¼ cup pure maple syrup
1½ teaspoons ground cinnamon
1 teaspoon ground nutmeg
½ teaspoon salt
    Maple Pecan Glaze (recipe follows)

1. Preheat oven to 325°F. Combine graham cracker crumbs, sugar and butter; press firmly on bottom of ungreased 9-inch springform pan.

2. In large bowl, beat cream cheese until fluffy. Gradually beat in EAGLE BRAND® until smooth. Add pumpkin, eggs, maple syrup, cinnamon, nutmeg and salt; mix well. Pour into crust.

3. Bake 1 hour and 15 minutes or until center appears nearly set when shaken. Cool 1 hour. Cover and chill at least 4 hours. Top with chilled Maple Pecan Glaze. Store leftovers covered in refrigerator.

Makes one (9-inch) cheesecake

Maple Pecan Glaze: In medium saucepan over medium-high heat, combine 1 cup (½ pint) whipping cream and ¾ cup pure maple syrup; bring to a boil. Boil rapidly 15 to 20 minutes or until thickened, stirring occasionally. Add ½ cup chopped pecans. Cover and chill. Stir before using.

Prep Time: 25 minutes
Bake Time: 1 hour and 15 minutes
Cool Time: 1 hour
Chill Time: 4 hours

Frozen Peppermint Cheesecake

   2 cups finely crushed chocolate wafer cookies or creme-filled
      chocolate sandwich cookies (about 24 cookies)
   ¼ cup sugar
   ¼ cup (½ stick) butter or margarine, melted
   1 (8-ounce) package cream cheese, softened
   1 (14-ounce) can EAGLE BRAND® Sweetened Condensed Milk
      (NOT evaporated milk)
   2 teaspoons peppermint extract
      Red food coloring (optional)
   2 cups whipping cream, whipped
      Hot fudge ice cream topping (optional)

1. In medium bowl, combine cookie crumbs and sugar. Add butter;
mix well. Press 2 cups crumb mixture firmly on bottom and halfway
up side of foil-lined 9-inch round cake or springform pan. Chill.

2. In large bowl, beat cream cheese until fluffy. Gradually beat in
EAGLE BRAND® until smooth. Stir in peppermint extract and food
coloring (optional); mix well. Fold in whipped cream. Pour into crust.

3. Cover; freeze 6 hours or until firm. Garnish with topping
(optional). Store leftovers covered in freezer.

Makes one (9-inch) cheesecake

Prep Time: *20 minutes*
Freeze Time: *6 hours*

Pumpkin Cheesecake Bars

1 (16-ounce) package pound cake mix
3 eggs, divided
2 tablespoons butter or margarine, melted
4 teaspoons pumpkin pie spice, divided
1 (8-ounce) package cream cheese, softened
1 (14-ounce) can EAGLE BRAND® Sweetened Condensed Milk
    (NOT evaporated milk)
1 (15-ounce) can pumpkin (2 cups)
½ teaspoon salt
1 cup chopped nuts

1. Preheat oven to 350°F. In large bowl with mixer on low speed, combine cake mix, 1 egg, butter and 2 teaspoons pumpkin pie spice until crumbly. Press on bottom of ungreased 15×10-inch jelly-roll pan.

2. In large bowl, beat cream cheese until fluffy. Gradually beat in EAGLE BRAND® until smooth. Beat in remaining 2 eggs, pumpkin, remaining 2 teaspoons pumpkin pie spice and salt; mix well.

3. Pour into prepared crust; sprinkle with nuts.

4. Bake 30 to 35 minutes or until set. Cool. Chill. Cut into bars. Store leftovers covered in refrigerator. *Makes 4 dozen bars*

Prep Time: 10 minutes
Bake Time: 30 to 35 minutes

Raspberry Swirl Cheesecakes

1½ cups fresh or frozen red raspberries, thawed
1 (14-ounce) can EAGLE BRAND® Sweetened Condensed Milk (NOT evaporated milk), divided
2 (8-ounce) packages cream cheese, softened
3 eggs
2 (6-ounce) prepared chocolate crumb pie crusts
Chocolate and white chocolate leaves (recipe follows, optional)
Fresh raspberries for garnish (optional)

1. Preheat oven to 350°F. In blender container, blend 1½ cups raspberries until smooth; press through sieve to remove seeds. Stir ⅓ cup EAGLE BRAND® into raspberry purée; set aside.

2. In large bowl, beat cream cheese until fluffy. Gradually beat in remaining EAGLE BRAND® until smooth. Add eggs; mix well. Pour into crusts. Drizzle with raspberry mixture. With knife, gently swirl raspberry mixture through cream cheese mixture.

3. Bake 25 minutes or until centers are nearly set when shaken. Cool. Cover and chill at least 4 hours. Garnish with chocolate leaves and fresh raspberries (optional). Store leftovers covered in refrigerator.

Makes two (9-inch) cheesecakes

Chocolate Leaves: Place 1 (1-ounce) square semisweet or white chocolate in microwave-safe bowl. Microwave on HIGH (100% power) 1 to 2 minutes, stirring every minute until smooth. With small, clean paintbrush, paint several coats of melted chocolate on undersides of nontoxic leaves, such as mint, lemon or strawberry. Wipe off any chocolate from top sides of leaves. Place leaves, chocolate sides up, on wax paper-lined baking sheet or on curved surface, such as rolling pin. Refrigerate leaves until chocolate is firm. To use, carefully peel leaves away from chocolate.

Prep Time: *15 minutes*
Bake Time: *25 minutes*
Chill Time: *4 hours*

Black & White Cheesecake

2 (3-ounce) packages cream cheese, softened
**1 (14-ounce) can EAGLE BRAND® Sweetened Condensed Milk
    (NOT evaporated milk)**
1 egg
1 teaspoon vanilla extract
½ cup miniature semisweet chocolate chips
1 teaspoon all-purpose flour
1 (6-ounce) prepared chocolate crumb pie crust
Chocolate Glaze (recipe follows)

1. Preheat oven to 350°F.

2. In medium bowl, beat cream cheese until fluffy. Gradually beat in EAGLE BRAND® until smooth. Add egg and vanilla; mix well.

3. In small bowl, toss chocolate chips with flour to coat; stir into cream cheese mixture. Pour into crust.

4. Bake 35 minutes or until center springs back when lightly touched. Cool. Prepare Chocolate Glaze and spread over cheesecake. Chill. Store leftovers covered in refrigerator.

Makes one (9-inch) cheesecake

Chocolate Glaze: In small saucepan over low heat, melt ½ cup miniature semisweet chocolate chips with ¼ cup whipping cream. Cook and stir until thickened and smooth. Use immediately.

Prep Time: 15 minutes
Bake Time: 35 minutes

Mini Cheesecakes

1½ cups graham cracker or chocolate wafer cookie crumbs
¼ cup sugar
¼ cup (½ stick) butter or margarine, melted
3 (8-ounce) packages cream cheese, softened
1 (14-ounce) can EAGLE BRAND® Sweetened Condensed Milk
   (NOT evaporated milk)
3 eggs
2 teaspoons vanilla extract

1. Preheat oven to 300°F. In small bowl, combine graham cracker crumbs, sugar and butter; press equal portions firmly on bottoms of 24 lightly greased or foil-lined muffin cups.

2. In large bowl, beat cream cheese until fluffy. Gradually beat in EAGLE BRAND® until smooth. Add eggs and vanilla; mix well. Spoon equal amounts of mixture (about 3 tablespoons) into prepared crusts.

3. Bake 20 minutes or until cheesecakes spring back when lightly touched. Cool.* Chill. Garnish as desired. Store leftovers covered in refrigerator.   *Makes 2 dozen mini cheesecakes*

If greased muffin cups are used, cool baked cheesecakes in pan. Freeze 15 minutes; remove with narrow spatula. Proceed as directed above.

Chocolate Mini Cheesecakes: Melt 1 cup (6 ounces) semisweet chocolate chips; mix into batter. Proceed as directed above, baking 20 to 25 minutes.

Prep Time: *20 minutes*
Bake Time: *20 minutes*

Creamy Baked Cheesecake

1¼ cups graham cracker crumbs
⅓ cup butter or margarine, melted
¼ cup sugar
2 (8-ounce) packages cream cheese, softened
1 (14-ounce) can EAGLE BRAND® Sweetened Condensed Milk
  (NOT evaporated milk)
3 eggs
¼ cup lemon juice
1 (8-ounce) container sour cream, at room temperature
  Raspberry Topping (page 45, optional)

1. Preheat oven to 300°F. In small bowl, combine graham cracker crumbs, butter and sugar; press firmly on bottom of ungreased 9-inch springform pan.

2. In large bowl, beat cream cheese until fluffy. Gradually beat in EAGLE BRAND® until smooth. Add eggs and lemon juice; mix well. Pour into prepared crust.

3. Bake 50 to 55 minutes or until set. Remove from oven; top with sour cream. Bake 5 minutes longer. Cool. Chill. Prepare Raspberry Topping (optional) and serve with cheesecake. Store leftovers covered in refrigerator.   *Makes one (9-inch) cheesecake*

New York Style Cheesecake: Increase cream cheese to 4 (8-ounce) packages and eggs to 4. Proceed as directed, adding 2 tablespoons flour after eggs. Bake 1 hour and 10 minutes or until center is set. Omit sour cream. Cool. Chill. Serve and store as directed.

Prep Time: 25 minutes
Bake Time: 55 to 60 minutes
Chill Time: 4 hours

Raspberry Topping

2 cups water
½ cup powdered sugar
¼ cup red raspberry jam
1 tablespoon cornstarch
1 cup frozen red raspberries

In small saucepan over medium heat, combine water, powdered sugar, jam and cornstarch. Cook and stir until thickened and clear. Cool. Stir in raspberries.

Prep Time: 5 minutes

Frozen Mocha Cheesecake Loaf

**2 cups finely crushed creme-filled chocolate sandwich cookies
(about 24 cookies)**
3 tablespoons butter or margarine, melted
1 (8-ounce) package cream cheese, softened
**1 (14-ounce) can EAGLE BRAND® Sweetened Condensed Milk
(NOT evaporated milk)**
1 tablespoon vanilla extract
2 cups (1 pint) whipping cream, whipped
2 tablespoons instant coffee
1 tablespoon hot water
½ cup chocolate syrup

1. Line 9×5-inch loaf pan with foil, extending foil over sides of pan.
In small bowl, combine cookie crumbs and butter; press firmly on
bottom and halfway up sides of prepared pan.

2. In large bowl, beat cream cheese until fluffy. Gradually beat
in EAGLE BRAND® until smooth. Stir in vanilla; mix well. Fold in
whipped cream.

3. Remove half the mixture and place in medium bowl. In small
bowl, dissolve coffee in water. Fold in coffee mixture and chocolate
syrup. Spoon half the chocolate mixture into prepared crust, then half
the vanilla mixture. Repeat. With knife, cut through cream mixture to
marble.

4. Cover; freeze 6 hours or until firm. To serve, remove from pan; peel
off foil. Cut into slices and garnish as desired. Store leftovers covered
in freezer.   *Makes one (9×5-inch) loaf*

Prep Time: 20 minutes
Freeze Time: 6 hours

Pies & Tarts

Banana Coconut Cream Pie

3 tablespoons cornstarch
1⅓ cups water
1 (14-ounce) can EAGLE BRAND® Sweetened Condensed Milk
   (NOT evaporated milk)
3 egg yolks, beaten
2 tablespoons butter or margarine
1 teaspoon vanilla extract
½ cup flaked coconut, toasted
2 medium bananas
2 tablespoons lemon juice
1 (9-inch) prepared graham cracker or baked pie crust
   Whipped cream and toasted coconut for garnish (optional)

1. In heavy saucepan over medium heat, dissolve cornstarch in water; stir in EAGLE BRAND® and egg yolks. Cook and stir until thickened and bubbly. Remove from heat; stir in butter and vanilla. Cool slightly. Fold in coconut; set aside.

2. Peel and slice bananas into ¼-inch-thick rounds. Toss banana slices gently with lemon juice; drain. Arrange bananas on bottom of crust. Pour filling over bananas.

3. Cover; refrigerate 4 hours or until set. Top with whipped cream and additional toasted coconut (optional). Store leftovers covered in refrigerator.

Makes one (9-inch) pie

Prep Time: *15 minutes*
Chill Time: *4 hours*

Perfect Pumpkin Pie

1 (15-ounce) can pumpkin (about 2 cups)
1 (14-ounce) can EAGLE BRAND® Sweetened Condensed Milk
   (NOT evaporated milk)
2 eggs
1 teaspoon ground cinnamon
½ teaspoon ground ginger
½ teaspoon ground nutmeg
½ teaspoon salt
1 (9-inch) unbaked pie crust

1. Preheat oven to 425°F.

2. In medium bowl, whisk pumpkin, EAGLE BRAND®, eggs, cinnamon, ginger, nutmeg and salt until smooth. Pour into crust. Bake 15 minutes.

3. Reduce oven temperature to 350°F and continue baking 35 to 40 minutes longer or until knife inserted 1 inch from crust comes out clean. Cool. Garnish as desired. Store leftovers covered in refrigerator.

Makes one (9-inch) pie

Sour Cream Topping: In medium bowl, combine 1½ cups sour cream, 2 tablespoons granulated sugar and 1 teaspoon vanilla extract. After pie has baked 30 minutes at 350°F, spread mixture evenly over top; bake 10 minutes longer.

Streusel Topping: In medium bowl, combine ½ cup packed brown sugar and ½ cup all-purpose flour; cut in ¼ cup (½ stick) cold butter or margarine until crumbly. Stir in ¼ cup chopped nuts. After pie has baked 30 minutes at 350°F, sprinkle streusel evenly over top; bake 10 minutes longer.

Chocolate Glaze: In small saucepan over low heat, melt ½ cup semisweet chocolate chips and 1 teaspoon solid shortening. Drizzle or spread over top of baked pie.

Prep Time: *15 minutes*
Bake Time: *50 to 55 minutes*

Apple Cranberry Streusel Custard Pie

1 (14-ounce) can EAGLE BRAND® Sweetened Condensed Milk (NOT evaporated milk)
1 teaspoon ground cinnamon
2 eggs, beaten
¹/₂ cup hot water
1¹/₂ cups fresh or frozen cranberries
2 medium all-purpose apples, peeled and sliced (about 1¹/₂ cups)
1 (9-inch) unbaked pie crust
¹/₂ cup firmly packed light brown sugar
¹/₂ cup all-purpose flour
¹/₄ cup (¹/₂ stick) butter or margarine, softened
¹/₂ cup chopped nuts

1. Place rack in lower third of oven; preheat oven to 425°F.

2. In large bowl, combine EAGLE BRAND® and cinnamon. Add eggs, water and fruits; mix well. Pour into crust.

3. In medium bowl, combine brown sugar and flour; cut in butter until crumbly. Add nuts. Sprinkle over pie. Bake 10 minutes.

4. Reduce oven temperature to 375°F; continue baking 30 to 40 minutes or until golden brown. Cool. Store covered in refrigerator.

Makes one (9-inch) pie

Prep Time: 25 minutes
Bake Time: 40 to 50 minutes

Key Lime Pie

3 eggs, separated
1 (14-ounce) can EAGLE BRAND® Sweetened Condensed Milk
    (NOT evaporated milk)
½ cup key lime juice
2 to 3 drops green food coloring (optional)
1 (9-inch) unbaked pie crust
¼ teaspoon cream of tartar
⅓ cup sugar

1. Preheat oven to 325°F.

2. In medium bowl, beat egg yolks; gradually beat in EAGLE BRAND® and lime juice. Stir in food coloring (optional). Pour into pie crust. Bake 30 minutes. Remove from oven. Increase oven temperature to 350°F.

3. In large bowl, beat egg whites and cream of tartar on high speed until soft peaks form. Gradually beat in sugar on medium speed, 1 tablespoon at a time; beat 4 minutes or until sugar is dissolved and stiff glossy peaks form.

4. Immediately spread meringue over hot pie, carefully sealing to edge of crust to prevent meringue from shrinking. Bake 15 minutes. Cool 1 hour. Chill at least 3 hours. Store leftovers covered in refrigerator. *Makes one (9-inch) pie*

Prep Time: 10 minutes
Bake Time: 45 minutes
Cool Time: 1 hour
Chill Time: 3 hours

Sweet Potato Pecan Pie

1 pound sweet potatoes or yams, cooked and peeled
¼ cup (½ stick) butter or margarine, softened
1 (14-ounce) can EAGLE BRAND® Sweetened Condensed Milk
    (NOT evaporated milk)
1 egg
1 teaspoon freshly grated orange rind
1 teaspoon ground cinnamon
1 teaspoon vanilla extract
½ teaspoon ground nutmeg
¼ teaspoon salt
1 (6-ounce) prepared graham cracker pie crust
    Pecan Topping (recipe follows)

1. Preheat oven to 425°F.

2. In large bowl, beat hot sweet potatoes and butter until smooth.
Add EAGLE BRAND®, egg, orange rind, cinnamon, vanilla, nutmeg
and salt; mix well. Pour into crust. Bake 20 minutes.

3. Meanwhile, prepare Pecan Topping.

4. Remove pie from oven; reduce oven temperature to 350°F. Spoon
Pecan Topping over pie.

5. Bake 25 minutes longer or until set. Cool. Serve warm or at room
temperature. Store leftovers covered in refrigerator.

Makes one (9-inch) pie

Pecan Topping: In small bowl, beat 1 egg, 2 tablespoons firmly packed
light brown sugar, 2 tablespoons dark corn syrup, 1 tablespoon melted
butter and ½ teaspoon maple flavoring. Stir in 1 cup chopped pecans.

Prep Time: *30 minutes*
Bake Time: *45 minutes*

Heavenly Chocolate Mousse Pie

4 (1-ounce) squares unsweetened chocolate, melted
1 (14-ounce) can EAGLE BRAND® Sweetened Condensed Milk
   (NOT evaporated milk)
1½ teaspoons vanilla extract
1 cup (½ pint) whipping cream, whipped
1 (6-ounce) prepared chocolate crumb pie crust

1. In large bowl, beat chocolate with EAGLE BRAND® and vanilla until well blended.

2. Chill 15 minutes or until cool; stir until smooth. Fold in whipped cream. Pour into crust.

3. Chill thoroughly. Garnish as desired. Store leftovers covered in refrigerator.

Makes one (9-inch) pie

Prep Time: *20 minutes*

Lemon Icebox Pie

1 (14-ounce) can EAGLE BRAND® Sweetened Condensed Milk (NOT evaporated milk)
½ cup lemon juice
   Yellow food coloring (optional)
1 cup (½ pint) whipping cream, whipped
1 (6-ounce) prepared graham cracker or baked pie crust

1. In medium bowl, combine EAGLE BRAND®, lemon juice and food coloring (optional). Fold in whipped cream. Pour into crust.

2. Chill 3 hours or until set. Garnish as desired. Store leftovers covered in refrigerator. *Makes one (9-inch) pie*

Prep Time: *10 minutes*
Chill Time: *3 hours*

Cranberry Crumb Pie

1 (9-inch) unbaked pie crust
1 (8-ounce) package cream cheese, softened
1 (14-ounce) can EAGLE BRAND® Sweetened Condensed Milk
    (NOT evaporated milk)
¼ cup lemon juice
3 tablespoons light brown sugar, divided
2 tablespoons cornstarch
1 (16-ounce) can whole berry cranberry sauce
¼ cup (½ stick) cold butter or margarine
⅓ cup all-purpose flour
¾ cup chopped walnuts

1. Preheat oven to 425°F. Bake pie crust 6 minutes; remove from oven. Reduce oven temperature to 375°F.

2. In large bowl, beat cream cheese until fluffy. Gradually beat in EAGLE BRAND® until smooth. Add lemon juice; mix well. Pour into baked crust.

3. In small bowl, combine 1 tablespoon brown sugar and cornstarch; mix well. Stir in cranberry sauce. Spoon evenly over cheese mixture.

4. In medium bowl, cut butter into flour and remaining 2 tablespoons brown sugar until crumbly. Stir in walnuts. Sprinkle evenly over cranberry mixture.

5. Bake 45 to 50 minutes or until bubbly and golden. Cool. Serve at room temperature or chill. Store leftovers covered in refrigerator.

Makes one (9-inch) pie

Prep Time: 20 minutes
Bake Time: 51 to 56 minutes

Decadent Brownie Pie

1 (9-inch) unbaked pie crust
1 cup (6 ounces) semisweet chocolate chips
¼ cup (½ stick) butter or margarine
1 (14-ounce) can EAGLE BRAND® Sweetened Condensed Milk
    (NOT evaporated milk)
½ cup biscuit baking mix
2 eggs
1 teaspoon vanilla extract
1 cup chopped nuts
Vanilla ice cream (optional)

1. Preheat oven to 375°F. Bake pie crust 10 minutes; remove from oven. Reduce oven temperature to 325°F.

2. In small saucepan over low heat, melt chocolate chips with butter.

3. In large bowl, beat chocolate mixture, EAGLE BRAND®, biscuit mix, eggs and vanilla until smooth. Stir in nuts. Pour into prepared pie crust.

4. Bake 40 to 45 minutes or until center is set. Cool at least 1 hour. Serve warm or at room temperature with ice cream (optional). Store leftovers covered in refrigerator.   *Makes one (9-inch) pie*

Prep Time: 20 minutes
Bake Time: 50 to 55 minutes
Cool Time: 1 hour

Chocolate Pie

1 (14-ounce) can EAGLE BRAND® Sweetened Condensed Milk
  (NOT evaporated milk)
2 (1-ounce) squares unsweetened chocolate
¼ teaspoon salt
¼ cup hot water
½ teaspoon vanilla extract
1 cup whipping cream, whipped
1 (9-inch) baked pie crust, cooled
  Additional whipped cream, shaved chocolate or chopped nuts
  (optional)

1. In top of double boiler, combine EAGLE BRAND®, chocolate and salt. Cook over hot water, stirring constantly, until mixture is very thick. Gradually add ¼ cup water, stirring constantly to keep mixture smooth. Continue to cook and stir 2 to 5 minutes or until mixture thickens again. Remove from heat. Stir in vanilla.

2. Chill mixture in refrigerator until cool; fold in whipped cream. Pour into baked crust. Refrigerate 4 hours.

3. Garnish with additional whipped cream, shaved chocolate or chopped nuts (optional). Store leftovers covered in refrigerator.

Makes one (9-inch) pie

Prep Time: 15 minutes

Peanut Butter Pie

Chocolate Crunch Crust (recipe follows)
1 **(8-ounce) package cream cheese, softened**
1 **(14-ounce) can EAGLE BRAND® Sweetened Condensed Milk**
 (NOT evaporated milk)
¾ **cup creamy peanut butter**
2 **tablespoons lemon juice**
1 **teaspoon vanilla extract**
1 **cup whipping cream, whipped *or* 1 (4-ounce) container frozen**
 non-dairy whipped topping, thawed
Chocolate fudge ice cream topping

1. Prepare Chocolate Crunch Crust.

2. In large bowl, beat cream cheese until fluffy. Gradually beat in
EAGLE BRAND® and peanut butter until smooth. Add lemon juice
and vanilla; mix well. Fold in whipped cream. Spread mixture in
baked crust.

3. Drizzle topping over pie. Refrigerate 4 to 5 hours or until firm.
Store leftovers covered in refrigerator.   *Makes one (9-inch) pie*

Chocolate Crunch Crust: In heavy saucepan over low heat, melt ⅓ cup
butter or margarine and 1 (6-ounce) package semisweet chocolate
chips. Remove from heat; gently stir in 2½ cups oven-toasted rice
cereal until completely coated. Press on bottom and up side to rim
of buttered 9-inch pie plate. Chill 30 minutes.

Prep Time: 20 minutes
Chill Time: 4 to 5 hours

Fudgy Pecan Pie

- ¼ cup (½ stick) butter or margarine
- 2 (1-ounce) squares unsweetened chocolate
- 1 (14-ounce) can EAGLE BRAND® Sweetened Condensed Milk (NOT evaporated milk)
- ½ cup hot water
- 2 eggs, well beaten
- 1¼ cups pecan halves or pieces
- 1 teaspoon vanilla extract
- ⅛ teaspoon salt
- 1 (9-inch) unbaked pie crust

1. Preheat oven to 350°F.

2. In medium saucepan over low heat, melt butter and chocolate. Stir in EAGLE BRAND®, hot water and eggs; mix well. Remove from heat; stir in pecans, vanilla and salt. Pour into crust.

3. Bake 40 to 45 minutes or until center is set. Cool slightly. Serve warm or chilled. Garnish as desired. Store leftovers covered in refrigerator.

Makes one (9-inch) pie

Prep Time: *15 minutes*
Bake Time: *40 to 45 minutes*

Chocolate Truffle Pie

- 1 envelope unflavored gelatin
- ½ cup water
- 3 (1-ounce) squares unsweetened or semisweet chocolate, melted and cooled
- 1 (14-ounce) can EAGLE BRAND® Sweetened Condensed Milk (NOT evaporated milk)
- 1 teaspoon vanilla extract
- 2 cups (1 pint) whipping cream, whipped
- 1 (6-ounce) prepared chocolate crumb pie crust

1. In small saucepan, sprinkle gelatin over water; let stand 1 minute. Over low heat, stir until gelatin dissolves.

2. In large bowl, beat chocolate and EAGLE BRAND® until smooth. Stir in gelatin mixture and vanilla. Fold in whipped cream. Pour into prepared crust.

3. Chill 3 hours or until set. Garnish as desired. Store leftovers covered in refrigerator.   *Makes one (9-inch) pie*

Prep Time: *15 minutes*
Chill Time: *3 hours*

Desserts

Peach Cream Cake

1 (10¾-ounce) loaf angel food cake, frozen
1 (14-ounce) can EAGLE BRAND® Sweetened Condensed Milk
(NOT evaporated milk)
1 cup cold water
1 teaspoon almond extract
1 (4-serving size) package instant vanilla pudding and pie
filling mix
2 cups (1 pint) whipping cream, whipped
4 cups sliced peeled fresh peaches (about 2 pounds)

1. Cut cake into ¼-inch slices; arrange half of slices on bottom of ungreased 13×9-inch baking dish.

2. In large bowl, combine EAGLE BRAND®, water and almond extract. Add pudding mix; beat well. Chill 5 minutes.

3. Fold in whipped cream. Spread half of cream mixture over cake slices; arrange half of peach slices on top. Top with remaining cake slices, cream filling and peach slices.

4. Chill 4 hours or until set. Cut into squares to serve. Store leftovers covered in refrigerator.   *Makes one (13×9-inch) cake*

Prep Time: 25 minutes
Chill Time: 4 hours and 5 minutes

Fudgy Milk Chocolate Fondue

1 (16-ounce) can chocolate syrup
1 (14-ounce) can EAGLE BRAND® Sweetened Condensed Milk
(NOT evaporated milk)
Dash salt
1½ teaspoons vanilla extract
Assorted dippers: cookies, cake cubes, pound cake cubes, angel
food cake cubes, banana chunks, apple slices, strawberries,
pear slices, kiwifruit slices and/or marshmallows

1. In heavy saucepan over medium heat, combine chocolate syrup, EAGLE BRAND® and salt. Cook and stir 12 to 15 minutes or until slightly thickened. Remove from heat; stir in vanilla.

2. Serve warm with assorted dippers. Store leftovers covered in refrigerator.   *Makes about 3 cups fondue*

Microwave Directions: In 1-quart glass measure, combine syrup, EAGLE BRAND® and salt. Microwave at HIGH (100% power) 3½ to 4 minutes, stirring after 2 minutes. Stir in vanilla.

Tip: Can be served warm or cold over ice cream. Can be made several weeks ahead. Store tightly covered in refrigerator.

Prep Time: *12 to 15 minutes*

Cherry-Berry Crumble

1 (21-ounce) can cherry pie filling
2 cups fresh or frozen raspberries
1 (14-ounce) can EAGLE BRAND® Sweetened Condensed Milk
    (NOT evaporated milk)
 1½ cups granola

1. In medium saucepan over medium heat, cook and stir cherry pie filling and raspberries until heated through. Stir in EAGLE BRAND®; cook and stir 1 minute.

2. Spoon into 6 individual dessert dishes or ungreased 2-quart square baking dish. Sprinkle with granola; garnish as desired. Serve warm. Store leftovers covered in refrigerator.   *Makes 6 servings*

Peach-Berry Crumble: Substitute peach pie filling for cherry pie filling.

Cherry-Rhubarb Crumble: Substitute fresh or frozen sliced rhubarb for raspberries. In medium saucepan over medium-high heat, cook and stir pie filling and rhubarb until bubbly. Cook and stir 5 minutes more. Proceed as directed above.

Prep Time: 10 minutes

Tiramisu

2 tablespoons instant coffee
½ cup hot water
2 (3-ounce) packages ladyfingers (24 each), cut crosswise into quarters
1 (14-ounce) can EAGLE BRAND® Sweetened Condensed Milk (NOT evaporated milk), divided
1 package (8 ounces) cream cheese or mascarpone, softened
2 cups (1 pint) whipping cream, divided
1 teaspoon vanilla extract
1 cup (6 ounces) miniature semisweet chocolate chips, divided
Grated semisweet chocolate and/or strawberries (optional)

1. In small bowl, dissolve coffee in water; reserve 1 tablespoon coffee mixture. Brush remaining coffee mixture on cut sides of ladyfingers; set aside.

2. In large bowl, beat ¾ cup EAGLE BRAND® and cream cheese. Add 1¼ cups whipping cream, vanilla and reserved 1 tablespoon coffee mixture; beat until soft peaks form. Fold in ½ cup chocolate chips.

3. In small heavy saucepan over low heat, melt remaining ½ cup chocolate chips with remaining EAGLE BRAND®.

4. In 8 individual tall dessert glasses or parfait glasses, layer cream cheese mixture, chocolate mixture and ladyfinger pieces, beginning and ending with cream cheese mixture.

5. Cover and chill at least 4 hours. In medium bowl, beat remaining ¾ cup cream until soft peaks form. Spoon whipped cream over dessert. Garnish as desired. Store leftovers covered in refrigerator.

Makes 8 servings

Prep Time: 30 minutes
Chill Time: 4 hours

Frozen Lemon Squares

1¼ cups graham cracker crumbs
¼ cup sugar
¼ cup (½ stick) butter or margarine, melted
3 egg yolks
1 (14-ounce) can EAGLE BRAND® Sweetened Condensed Milk
    (NOT evaporated milk)
½ cup lemon juice
    Yellow food coloring (optional)
    Whipped cream or non-dairy whipped topping

1. Preheat oven to 325°F. In small bowl, combine graham cracker crumbs, sugar and butter; press firmly on bottom of ungreased 8- or 9-inch square baking pan. Bake 8 minutes.

2. In small bowl, beat egg yolks, EAGLE BRAND®, lemon juice and food coloring (optional). Pour over hot crust.

3. Bake 30 minutes. Cool completely. Top with whipped cream.

4. Freeze 4 hours or until firm. Let stand 10 minutes before serving. Garnish as desired. Store leftovers covered in freezer.

Makes 6 to 9 squares

Prep Time: *15 minutes*
Bake Time: *30 minutes*
Freeze Time: *4 hours*

Creamy Banana Pudding

 1 (14-ounce) can EAGLE BRAND® Sweetened Condensed Milk
    (NOT evaporated milk)
1½ cups cold water
 1 (4-serving size) package instant vanilla pudding and pie filling
    mix
 2 cups (1 pint) whipping cream, whipped
36 vanilla wafers
 3 medium bananas, sliced and dipped in lemon juice

1. In large bowl, combine EAGLE BRAND® and water. Add pudding mix; beat until well blended. Chill 5 minutes.

2. Fold in whipped cream. Spoon 1 cup pudding mixture into 2½-quart glass serving bowl or divide it among 8 to 10 individual serving dishes.

3. Top with one third each vanilla wafers, bananas and pudding mixture. Repeat layers twice, ending with pudding mixture. Chill. Garnish as desired. Store leftovers covered in refrigerator.

Makes 8 to 10 servings

Prep Time: *15 minutes*

Double Chocolate Ice Cream Squares

1½ cups finely crushed creme-filled chocolate sandwich cookies
   (about 18 cookies)
2 to 3 tablespoons butter or margarine, melted
1 (14-ounce) can EAGLE BRAND® Sweetened Condensed Milk
   (NOT evaporated milk)
3 (1-ounce) squares unsweetened chocolate, melted
2 teaspoons vanilla extract
1 cup chopped nuts (optional)
2 cups (1 pint) whipping cream, whipped
   Whipped topping
   Additional chopped nuts (optional)

1. In medium bowl, combine cookie crumbs and butter; press firmly on bottom of ungreased 13×9-inch baking pan.

2. In large bowl, beat EAGLE BRAND®, melted chocolate and vanilla until well blended. Stir in nuts (optional). Fold in whipped cream. Pour into crust. Spread with whipped topping.

3. Cover; freeze 6 hours or until firm. Garnish with additional chopped nuts (optional) or as desired. Store leftovers covered in freezer.   *Makes about 1 dozen squares*

Rocky Road Ice Cream Squares: Add 1 cup miniature marshmallows to EAGLE BRAND® mixture. Proceed as directed above.

Prep Time: 20 minutes
Freeze Time: 6 hours

Date and Nut Roll

2 cups vanilla wafer crumbs
1 cup chopped dates
½ cup chopped nuts
½ cup EAGLE BRAND® Sweetened Condensed Milk
   (NOT evaporated milk)
2 teaspoons lemon juice from concentrate

1. In large bowl, combine wafer crumbs, dates and nuts. In small bowl, combine EAGLE BRAND® and lemon juice. Add to crumb mixture and knead well. Form into roll (3 inches in diameter) and cover with waxed paper. Chill in refrigerator 12 hours or longer.

2. Cut chilled roll into slices. Garnish with whipped cream or drizzle leftover EAGLE BRAND® over slices.   *Makes 8 servings*

Chocolate Peanut Butter Dessert Sauce

- **2 (1-ounce) squares semisweet chocolate, chopped**
- **2 tablespoons creamy peanut butter**
- **1 (14-ounce) can EAGLE BRAND® Sweetened Condensed Milk (NOT evaporated milk)**
- **2 tablespoons milk**
- **1 teaspoon vanilla extract**
  Fresh fruit, ice cream or cake

1. In medium saucepan over medium-low heat, melt chocolate and peanut butter with EAGLE BRAND® and milk, stirring constantly. Remove from heat; stir in vanilla. Cool slightly.

2. Serve warm as fruit dipping sauce or over ice cream or cake. Store leftovers covered in refrigerator. *Makes about 1½ cups sauce*

Prep Time: 15 minutes

Creamy Caramel Flan

¾ **cup sugar**
4 **eggs**
1¾ **cups water**
1 **(14-ounce) can EAGLE BRAND® Sweetened Condensed Milk**
   (NOT evaporated milk)
1 **teaspoon vanilla extract**
   Dash salt
   Sugar Garnish (recipe follows, optional)

1. Preheat oven to 350°F. In medium heavy skillet over medium heat, cook and stir sugar until melted and caramel-colored. Carefully pour into 8 ungreased 6-ounce custard cups, tilting to coat bottoms.

2. In large bowl, beat eggs; stir in water, EAGLE BRAND®, vanilla and salt. Pour into custard cups. Set cups in large deep pan. Fill pan with 1 inch hot water.

3. Bake 25 minutes or until knife inserted near centers comes out clean. Move cups from pan to wire rack. Cool 1 hour. Chill several hours or overnight.

4. To serve, loosen sides of flans with knife; invert flans onto individual serving plates. Top with Sugar Garnish (optional), or as desired. Store leftovers covered in refrigerator.

Makes 8 servings

Sugar Garnish: Fill medium metal bowl half-full of ice. In medium saucepan over medium-high heat, combine 1 cup granulated sugar with ¼ cup water. Stir; cover and bring to a boil. Cook over high heat 5 to 6 minutes or until light brown in color. Immediately place pan in ice for 1 minute. Using spoon, carefully drizzle sugar decoratively over foil. Cool. To serve, peel sugar garnish from foil.

Prep Time: *15 minutes*
Bake Time: *25 minutes*

Ambrosia Freeze

1 (8-ounce) container strawberry cream cheese
2 medium bananas, mashed
1 (14-ounce) can EAGLE BRAND® Sweetened Condensed Milk
  (NOT evaporated milk)
1 (8-ounce) container low-fat strawberry yogurt
2 tablespoons lemon juice
1 (11-ounce) can mandarin orange sections, drained
1 (8-ounce) can crushed pineapple, well drained
½ cup toasted flaked coconut
  Red food coloring (optional)

1. In large bowl with electric mixer on low speed, beat cream cheese and bananas until smooth. Beat in EAGLE BRAND®, yogurt and lemon juice until blended. Stir in orange sections, pineapple and coconut. Stir in food coloring (optional). Spoon into ungreased 11×7-inch baking dish.

2. Cover and freeze 6 hours or until firm. Remove from freezer 15 minutes before serving. Cut into 1×1-inch cubes; serve in stemmed glasses or dessert dishes. *Makes 8 to 10 servings*

Crunchy Peppermint Candy Ice Cream

2 cups (1 pint) light cream
1 (14-ounce) can EAGLE BRAND® Sweetened Condensed Milk (NOT evaporated milk)
1¼ cups water
½ cup crushed hard peppermint candy
1 tablespoon vanilla extract
Additional peppermint candy (optional)

1. Combine cream, EAGLE BRAND®, water, peppermint candy and vanilla in ice cream freezer container. Freeze according to manufacturer's instructions.

2. Garnish with additional peppermint candy (optional). Store leftovers tightly covered in freezer.   *Makes 1½ quarts*

Prep Time: 15 minutes

Candies & Treats

No-Bake Peanutty Chocolate Drops

½ cup (1 stick) butter or margarine
⅓ cup unsweetened cocoa
2½ cups quick-cooking oats
1 (14-ounce) can EAGLE BRAND® Sweetened Condensed Milk (NOT evaporated milk)
1 cup chopped peanuts
½ cup peanut butter

1. In medium saucepan over medium heat, melt butter; stir in cocoa. Bring mixture to a boil. Remove from heat; stir in oats, EAGLE BRAND®, peanuts and peanut butter.

2. Drop by teaspoonfuls onto wax paper-lined baking sheet. Chill 2 hours or until set. Store leftovers loosely covered in refrigerator.

Makes about 5 dozen drops

Prep Time: *10 minutes*
Chill Time: *2 hours*

Chilled Café Latte

   2 tablespoons instant coffee
   ¾ cup warm water
   1 (14-ounce) can EAGLE BRAND® Fat Free or Original Sweetened
      Condensed Milk (NOT evaporated milk)
   1 teaspoon vanilla extract
   4 cups ice cubes

1. In blender container, dissolve coffee in water. Add EAGLE BRAND®
and vanilla; cover and blend on high speed until smooth.

2. With blender running, gradually add ice cubes, blending until
smooth. Serve immediately. Store leftovers covered in refrigerator.

Makes about 5 cups

Prep Time: 10 minutes

Strawberry Splash Punch

1½ cups fresh whole strawberries
½ cup lemon juice, chilled
1 (14-ounce) can EAGLE BRAND® Sweetened Condensed Milk
(NOT evaporated milk), chilled
1 (1-liter) bottle strawberry carbonated beverage, chilled
Ice cubes (optional)
Fresh whole strawberries (optional)

1. In blender container, combine 1½ cups strawberries and lemon juice; cover and blend until smooth. Add EAGLE BRAND®; cover and blend. Pour into large pitcher.

2. Gradually stir in carbonated beverage. Add ice (optional). Garnish each serving with whole strawberry (optional).

Makes 10 servings

Prep Time: *10 minutes*

Creamy Cinnamon Rolls

2 (1-pound) loaves frozen bread dough, thawed
⅔ cup (half of 14-ounce can*) EAGLE BRAND® Sweetened
    Condensed Milk (NOT evaporated milk), divided
1 cup chopped pecans
2 teaspoons ground cinnamon
1 cup confectioners' sugar
½ teaspoon vanilla extract
    Additional chopped pecans (optional)

*Use remaining EAGLE BRAND® as a dip for fruit. Pour into storage
container and store tightly covered in refrigerator for up to 1 week.*

1. On lightly floured surface, roll each bread dough loaf into
12×9-inch rectangle. Spread ⅓ cup EAGLE BRAND® over dough
rectangles. Cover and chill remaining EAGLE BRAND®. Sprinkle
rectangles with 1 cup pecans and cinnamon. Roll up jelly-roll style
starting from short side. Cut each log into 6 slices.

2. Place rolls cut sides down in well greased 13×9-inch pan. Cover
loosely with greased wax paper and then with plastic wrap. Chill
overnight.

3. Let pan of rolls stand at room temperature 30 minutes. Preheat
oven to 350°F. Bake 30 to 35 minutes or until golden brown. Cool
in pan 5 minutes; loosen edges and remove rolls from pan.

4. In small bowl, combine confectioners' sugar, remaining ⅓ cup
EAGLE BRAND® and vanilla. Drizzle frosting over warm rolls.
Sprinkle with additional chopped pecans (optional).

Makes 12 rolls

Prep Time: 20 minutes
Chill Time: Overnight
Bake Time: 30 to 35 minutes
Cool Time: 5 minutes

Peanut Butter Fudge

2 (10-ounce) packages peanut butter-flavored chips
1 (14-ounce) can EAGLE BRAND® Sweetened Condensed Milk
(NOT evaporated milk)
¼ cup (½ stick) butter or margarine, cut into pieces
1 cup chopped salted peanuts
Additional chopped salted peanuts (optional)

1. Butter 8-inch square dish. In 2-quart microwave-safe bowl, combine peanut butter chips, EAGLE BRAND® and butter. Microwave at MEDIUM (50% power) 4 to 5 minutes, stirring at 1½-minute intervals.

2. Stir in peanuts and pour into prepared dish. Garnish with additional chopped peanuts (optional). Cover and chill 2 hours. Cut into squares. Store covered in refrigerator.

Makes 2 pounds fudge

Prep Time: *5 minutes*
Cook Time: *4 to 5 minutes*
Chill Time: *2 hours*

Chocolate Raspberry Truffles

1 (14-ounce) can EAGLE BRAND® Sweetened Condensed Milk (NOT evaporated milk)
¼ cup raspberry liqueur
2 tablespoons butter or margarine
2 tablespoons seedless raspberry jam
2 cups (12 ounces) semisweet chocolate chips
½ cup powdered sugar or finely chopped toasted almonds

1. In large microwave-safe bowl, combine EAGLE BRAND®, liqueur, butter and jam. Microwave on HIGH (100% power) 3 minutes.

2. Stir in chocolate chips until smooth. Cover and chill 1 hour.

3. Shape mixture into 1-inch balls; roll in powdered sugar or almonds. Store leftovers covered at room temperature.

Makes 4 dozen truffles

Prep Time: 10 minutes
Cook Time: 3 minutes
Chill Time: 1 hour

Chocolate Snow Swirl Fudge

   3 cups semisweet chocolate chips
   1 (14-ounce) can EAGLE BRAND® Sweetened Condensed Milk
     (NOT evaporated milk)
  ¼ cup (½ stick) butter or margarine, divided
    Dash salt
   1 cup chopped nuts
1½ teaspoons vanilla extract
   2 cups miniature marshmallows

1. In large heavy saucepan over low heat, melt chocolate chips with EAGLE BRAND®, 2 tablespoons butter and salt. Remove from heat; stir in nuts and vanilla. Spread evenly in wax paper-lined 8- or 9-inch square pan.

2. In small saucepan over low heat, melt marshmallows with remaining 2 tablespoons butter; stir until smooth. Spread on top of fudge. With knife or metal spatula, swirl through fudge to marble.

3. Chill at least 2 hours or until firm. Turn fudge onto cutting board; peel off paper and cut into squares. Store leftovers covered in refrigerator.   *Makes about 2 pounds fudge*

Prep Time: *30 minutes*
Chill Time: *2 hours*

S'mores on a Stick

1 (14-ounce) can EAGLE BRAND® Sweetened Condensed Milk (NOT evaporated milk), divided
1½ cups miniature milk chocolate chips, divided
1 cup miniature marshmallows
11 whole graham crackers, halved crosswise
Toppings: chopped peanuts, miniature candy-coated chocolate pieces, sprinkles

1. In microwave-safe bowl, microwave half of EAGLE BRAND® at HIGH (100% power) 1½ minutes. Stir in 1 cup chocolate chips until smooth; stir in marshmallows.

2. Spread chocolate mixture evenly by heaping tablespoonfuls onto 11 graham cracker halves. Top with remaining graham cracker halves; place on wax paper.

3. Microwave remaining EAGLE BRAND® at HIGH (100% power) 1½ minutes; stir in remaining ½ cup chocolate chips, stirring until smooth. Drizzle mixture over treats; sprinkle with desired toppings.

4. Let stand for 2 hours; insert wooden craft stick into centers.

Makes 11 treats

Prep Time: *10 minutes*
Cook Time: *3 minutes*

Candy Crunch

- **4 cups (half of 15-ounce bag) pretzel sticks or pretzel twists**
- **4 cups (24 ounces) white chocolate chips**
- **1 (14-ounce) can EAGLE BRAND® Sweetened Condensed Milk (NOT evaporated milk)**
- **1 cup dried fruit (dried cranberries, raisins or mixed dried fruit bits)**

1. Place pretzels in large bowl.

2. In large saucepan over low heat, melt white chocolate chips with EAGLE BRAND®. Cook and stir constantly until smooth. Pour over pretzels, stirring to coat.

3. Immediately spread mixture into foil-lined 15×10-inch jelly roll pan. Sprinkle with dried fruit; press down lightly with back of spoon. Chill 1 to 2 hours or until set. Break into chunks. Store leftovers loosely covered at room temperature.

Makes about 1¾ pounds candy

Prep Time: *10 minutes*
Chill Time: *1 to 2 hours*